POEMS 2

POEMS 2

ALAN DUGAN

New Haven and London: Yale University Press, 1963

Acknowledgment is made to the following publications for poems
which originally appeared in them:

Poetry (Chicago)

"Three as a Magic Number"

"To a Red-Headed Do-Good Waitress"

"Winter's Onset from an Alienated Point of View"

"Free Variation on a Translation from Greek"

"851"

"Fabrication of Ancestors"

"Admonition: A Pearl for Arrogance"

"From Heraclitus"

"On Trees"

"What the Hell, Rage, Give in to Natural Graces"

"Variation on a Theme by Stevens"

"Accommodation to Detroit"

Partisan Review

"For Masturbation"

Saturday Review

"Monologue of a Commercial Fisherman"

"In the Forest"

American Scholar

"Winter: For an Untenable Situation"

SPEKTRUM (Zürich)

"Romance of the Escaped Children"

translated into German by Annemarie Schönholzer

CONTENTS

Three as a Magic Number   3
Coat of Arms   4
Romance of the Escaped Children   6
Elegy   7
Two Quits and a Drum, and Elegy for Drinkers
    1. On Asphalt: No Greens   8
    2. Portrait against Women   9
    3. Courage. Exceed.   11
    4. Elegy for Drinkers   11
To a Red-Headed Do-Good Waitress   14
On a Seven-Day Diary   15
Elegy for a Gifted Child   16
    Counter-Elegy   16
Credo   18
Winter's Onset from an Alienated Point of View   19
On Hat: On Vertical Mobility as a Concept   20
On Trading Time for Life by Work   21
Free Variation on a Translation from Greek   22
The Repealer: "You're too Wild"   23
On Going Latent   24
For Masturbation   25
Fragment on the British Museum   26
On Breeding, from Plutarch   28
Poem   29
On an Accident: On a Newspaper Story   30
851   31
Fabrication of Ancestors   32
Autumn at Baiae: For Cavafy   33
Riding Song for a Semi-Feudal Army, for Glubb Pasha,
    for Tortured Colonels   34
Poem   36

On Lines 69–70, Book IV, of Virgil's *Aeneid*   37
Admonitor: A Pearl for Arrogance   38
General Prothalamion in Populous Times   40
The Crimes of Bernard   41
On Visiting Central Park Zoo   42
The Life and Death of the Cantata System   43
Plague of Dead Sharks   44
From Heraclitus   45
On Finding the Meaning of "Radiance"   46
A Gift's Accompaniment   47
Argument to Love as a Person   48
In the Forest   49
A Sawyer's Rage against Trees Noble as Horses   50
What the Hell, Rage, Give in to Natural Graces   52
On Trees: Secular Metamorphosis of Joyce Kilmer's
    "Trees"   54
Poem   55
Monologue of a Commercial Fisherman   56
Variation on a Theme by Stevens   57
From Rome. For More Public Fountains in New York
    City   58
Accommodation to Detroit   59
To Paris: Fear of the Heights Reached   60
Stability Before Departure   61
Winter: For an Untenable Situation   62

FOR JUDY

POEMS 2

THREE AS A MAGIC NUMBER

Three times dark, first in the mind,
second in January, the pit of the year,
and third in subways going up and down
the hills and valleys underground,
I go from indoors to indoors indoors,
seeing the Hudson River three times a week
from my analyst's penthouse window. It
is a brilliant enlargement three ways:
in and out and fluvial. The river goes
like white smoke from the industries
to the north, and the rigged-up lights
of the Palisades Amusement Park
promise a west of pleasure, open space,
and a circus of whippable lions,
while the cliffs beneath them, made
of latent vegetation, the live rock,
and a fall of snow, seems to me to be
the hanging gardens of Hammurabi.

COAT OF ARMS

In memory of E. A. Dugan

My father's Memory Book
was warm before the womb
among gymnasium smells
of resolutions put to dust.
The grand tour of his squint
that stopped for photographs
before each sepia Wonder
found Ithaca and ease
beneath the attic dust.
What a joker, like me:
he came into the womb
where I was, poked around
and spat and left and I
was forced out wet
into the cold air. Someone
slapped me and I wept
to have become a travelling man.
Oh I inherited his book
stamped with a coat of arms
self-made from dreams—
a moon and family beast,
a phrase around a shield
boldly nicked with feats
and warm before the womb—
and wondered, laughing, why,
when heroes have come home

4

from labors out of time
they loll out fatherhood
in baseball-worship, old
underclothes, odd sales jobs
and bad stories often told,
told often, stories often told,
but in one photograph,
the last before the womb,
the dragon had been stuffed
and shipped off home,
authentically killed, and he
is posed in mail, his head
fixed in a photographer's clamp
and Coney Island smile
graced by the cry: "INHIBIT!"
So I learned to rent arms too,
and go out broke without
escutcheon, with a blank
shield against all critics and
a motto of my own
devising on the rim:

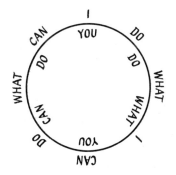

and throw down a left-handed glove
under the cry: "ETCETERA!"

ROMANCE OF THE
ESCAPED CHILDREN

Goodbye, children: the bad Good Knight
is through. The rescued girl is asleep,
dreaming of ransom and astrologers
in the highest room of the family Keep.

On the second floor the Him Himself
is sound asleep among his pudding wife
and in the great Ground Hall below
retainers denounce the family wine

and pick at the bones of a cold dwarf.
Down in the cellars you shivered about,
continuous shrieks applaud the rack: he is,
from top to bottom, a good to bad scout,

domestic in the middle. You are fortunate
to have escaped from this on muffled oars.

ELEGY

I know but will not tell
you, Aunt Irene, why there
are soap-suds in the whiskey:
Uncle Robert had to have
a drink while shaving. May
there be no bloodshed in your house
this morning of my father's death
and no unkept appearance
in the living, since he has
to wear the rouge and lipstick
of your ceremony, mother,
for the first and last time:
father, hello and goodbye.

TWO QUITS AND A DRUM, AND ELEGY FOR DRINKERS

1. ON ASPHALT: NO GREENS

Quarry out the stone
of land, cobble the beach,
wall surf, name it "street",
allow no ground or green
cover for animal sins,
but let opacity of sand
be glass to keep the heat
outside, the senses in.
Then, when time's Drunk,
reeling to death, provokes
god's favor as a fool,
oh let a lamp-post grow
out of its absence, bend,
heavy with care, and bloom
light. Let a curb extrude
a comfortable fault. Let
"street" become a living room.
Comfortably seated, lit
by the solicitude of "lamp",
the Drunk and street are one.
They say, "Let's have no dirt:
bulldoze the hills into
their valleys: make it plain.
Then take the mountains down
and let their decks of slate
be dealt out flat grey.

Let their mating seams
be tarred against the weeds
by asphalt, by the night's
elixir of volcanoes hotly poured."
Then the soulless port at night
is made a human, and the Drunk
god: no one else is here
to be so but who cares?

2. PORTRAIT AGAINST WOMEN

Bones, in his falling,
must have hit the skin
between themselves and stone,
but distances of wine
were his upholstery
against the painful crime
of lying in the street,
since "God protects them."
He rolled onto his back,
his right hand in his fly,
and gargled open-mouthed,
showing the white of an eye:
it did not see the sign
raised on the proper air
that read: "Here lies
a god-damned fool. Beware."

No: his hand, his woman, on
the dry root of his sex,
debates it: deformed by wine
and fantasy, the wreck
of infant memory is there,
of how the garden gate
slammed at the words, "Get
out you god-damned bum,"
and so he was, since she,
goddess, mother, and wife,
spoke and it was the fact.
Her living hair came out
gray in his hand, her teeth
went false at his kiss,
and her solid flesh went slack
like mother's. "Now, lady, I
am sick and out of socks,
so save me: I am pure although
my hand is on my cock."
Then he could rise up young
out of his vagrancy
in whole unwilled reform
and shuck the fallen one,
his furlough in this street
redeemed by her grace.
There would be the grass
to lay her on, the quench
of milk behind the taste of wine,
and laughter in a dreamed
jungle of love behind
a billboard that could read:
"This is YOUR Garden:
Please keep it clean."

3. COURAGE. EXCEED.

A beggar with no legs below
the middle of his knees
walked down Third Avenue
on padded sockets, on
his telescoped or
anti-stilted legs
repeating, "Oh beautiful
faspacious skies!," upon
a one-man band: a bass
drum on roller-skates,
a mouth-high bugle clamped
to it, and cymbals interlocked
inside a fate of noise. He
flew the American flag
for children on a stick
stuck in a veteran's hat,
and offered pencils. He
was made of drunks' red eyes.
He cried, "Courage! Exceed!"
He was collapsed in whole
display. Drunkards, for this
and with his pencil I
put down his words drunk:
"Stand! Improvise!"

4. ELEGY FOR DRINKERS

What happened to the drunks
I used to know, the prodigals
who tried their parents' help
too far? Some misers of health
have aged out dry; the rest

are sick and out of socks,
their skin-tight ankle-bones
blue as the mussel shells
that rolled in Naxos' surf
when Bacchus danced ashore
and kicked them all to hell.

> Oh gutter urinal,
> be Dirce's holy stream,
> so lightning out of Zeus
> can rage on Semele,
> invited! Permit her son,
> issuant of His thigh,
> to rule her family
> as Bromios, god of wine!

Oh Dionisos, good god
of memory and sleep,
you grace the paper bag,
stuck in the fork of a crutch,
that holds the secret sons
and furniture of bums,
since wine is the cure of wine.
It's thanks to you that I,
in my condition, am
still possible and praising: I
am drunk today, but what
about tomorrow? I burnt
my liver to you for a drink,
so pay me for my praises:
for thirty-seven cents, for
the price of a pint of lees,
I would praise wine, your name,
and how your trouble came

out of the east to Thebes:
you taught the women wine
and tricked King Pentheus
to mask as one of them:
because his father died
to all appeals for help,
the rending penalty,
death at his mother's hands!,
still fills The Bowery
with prodigals of hope:
they pray for lightning and
a dance to their god damn,
since wine is the cure of wine
and wine the cure wine cured
and wine the cure of wine.

TO A RED-HEADED DO-GOOD WAITRESS

Every morning I went to her charity and learned
to face the music of her white smile so well
that it infected my black teeth as I escaped,
and those who saw me smiled too and went in
the White Castle, where she is the inviolable lady.

There cripples must be bright, and starvers noble:
no tears, no stomach-cries, but pain made art
to move her powerful red pity toward philanthropy.
So I must wear my objectively stinking poverty
like a millionaire clown's rags and sing, "Oh I

got plenty o' nuttin'," as if I made
a hundred grand a year like Gershwin, while
I get a breakfast every day from her for two
weeks and nothing else but truth: she has
a policeman and a wrong sonnet in fifteen lines.

ON A SEVEN-DAY DIARY

Oh I got up and went to work
and worked and came back home
and ate and talked and went to sleep.
Then I got up and went to work
and worked and came back home
from work and ate and slept.
Then I got up and went to work
and worked and came back home
and ate and watched a show and slept.
Then I got up and went to work
and worked and came back home
and ate steak and went to sleep.
Then I got up and went to work
and worked and came back home
and ate and fucked and went to sleep.
Then it was Saturday, Saturday, Saturday!
Love must be the reason for the week!
We went shopping! I saw clouds!
The children explained everything!
I could talk about the main thing!
What did I drink on Saturday night
that lost the first, best half of Sunday?
The last half wasn't worth this "word."
Then I got up and went to work
and worked and came back home
from work and ate and went to sleep,
refreshed but tired by the week-end.

ELEGY FOR A GIFTED CHILD

Ephemeron! It's over! All
the scales of the clock-faces
are so heavy with life,
so loaded to capacity
with eyelids and lashes,
that they have come around again
to zero, midnight. Since you
were no Faust at noon,
no Mephistopheles at midnight
will reward your prayers with Hell
and its continuous distractions: it's
just all over, Ephemeron.

COUNTER-ELEGY

Oh no. I go on
doing what I have
to do because I do
it: I sat and sat
there counting one
plus one plus one
while all the rest
were somewhere else,
playing in the tripe
of a living horse
and stroking its great
eyes: this took time!
Then at the end
of that eternity

they gave me 60 bucks
less taxes and dues
and said, "Come back
tomorrow; there
is always work to do."
It was night! I went out!
Oh I got stewed,
screwed and tattooed!
My skin read: I LOVE
MY MOTHER in a heart
pierced by a naked sword!
Weak in the needling, it
was there for all life long
in the bent branch of my arm.
You think I just
went off like a bomb
and was over, but
it has seemed long to me,
slow as the explosion of
the whole life of the tree
in which the birds evolved,
each singing out its song.

CREDO

They told me, "You don't have
    to work: you can starve,"
so I walked off my job
    and went broke. All day
I looked for love and cash
    in the gutters and found
a pencil, paper, and a dime
    shining in the fading light,
so I ate, drank, and wrote:
    "It is no use: poverty
is worse than work, so why
    starve at liberty? when I
can eat as a slave, drink
    in the evening, and pay
for your free love at night."

WINTER'S ONSET FROM
AN ALIENATED POINT OF VIEW

The first cold front came in
whining like a carpenter's plane
and curled the warm air
up the sky: winter is
for busy work, summer
for construction. As for
spring and fall, ah, you
know what we do then:
sow and reap. I want
never to be idle or by plumb
or level to fear death,
so I do none of this
in offices away from weather.

ON HAT: ON VERTICAL MOBILITY
AS A CONCEPT

From the official hurry on the top floor
and through the irony on the working floors
down to the sleep stolen in the basement,
the company went on incorporate and firm,
drumming like an engine through the spring day.
Standing still but often going up and down
while breaking in a new winter felt hat,
the elevator operator was the best man in
the place in humor. Going from the thieves
at the top to the bums in the cellar
and past the tame working people in between,
he was denoting Plato's ideal form of Hat
vertically in an unjust state in the spring:
he did nothing but social service for nothing
as a form to be walked on like stairs.

ON TRADING
TIME FOR LIFE BY WORK

The receptionist has shiny fingernails
since she has buffed them up for hours,
not for profit but for art, while they,
the partners, have been arguing themselves
the further into ruthless paranoia,
the accountant said. The sales representatives
came out against the mustard yellow: "It
looks like baby-shit," and won, as ever. In
the studio, the artist, art-director, and
the copy-chief were wondering out loud:
Whether a "Peace On Earth" or a "Love
And Peace On Earth" should go around
the trumpeting angel on the Christmas card.
In this way the greeting card company
worked back and forth across a first spring
afternoon like a ferry-boat on the river:
time was passing, it itself was staying the same,
and workers rode it on the running depths
while going nowhere back and forth across
the surface of the river. Profits flow away
in this game, and thank god there is none
of the transcendence printed on the product.

FREE VARIATION ON A
TRANSLATION FROM GREEK

In times of peace and good government
there is increase of fruits and ease.
The house-spider tries to spin her web
from the air-raid helmet to the gun
in the closet, but quits at the sound
of the morning vacuum-cleaner: the sound
father keeps his weapons clean but locked away.
The afternoon is broad. The evening
is for supper and nothing. At night the ex-
soldier can wake from honey-hearted sleep
and turn to his own wife in his own
bed for a change, for solace against fears
of death by normal attrition. At 6 A.M.
there are no police knocking: his only problems,
besides the major ones of love, work, and death,
are noisy children: playing out in the street
before breakfast and against his rules, a joke
occurs, and their laughter starts, builds,
and then goes up like a prayer against the rules
and for the time of peace and good government
in which it happens: they could have lit
a used Christmas tree: it goes up in fire
but burns invisibly in the clear morning air
while roaring. Then he goes to work again,
instead of war, and the day stands as said.

THE REPEALER:
"YOU'RE TOO WILD"

You laughed with an open mouth
to show the flowering ivory
of your temporary teeth because
you hit him on the head hard
with a croquet mallet, drawing
real blood. Now I know you as
the laugher and the hammerer,
as Charles Martel The Churl
who comes to change the past
with blood and laughter. Don't
fall to the grief that makes
your father beat you up, but
encourage your essence! Be-
jewel your mallet and strike
for a world of growing joy.

ON GOING LATENT

Arcadia was square and fenced
with upright planks. It had
a slate path pretended as
a stream of square meander
which I hopped and helped
my mother May to cross.
Roses were tied to sticks
in dirty holes in the grass.
Once I saw a snake
and ran away indoors,
crying of hell, and stopped
her conversation with an aunt.
Armored in women, I
returned and found the worm
groveling in laughter: it
had crucified the roses and
had made a fool of snakes
before I did or did not
stamp it out. I fell asleep
and did not wake up later,
until I woke up far away
and worked to be your lover.

FOR MASTURBATION

I have allowed myself
this corner and am God.
Here in the must
beneath their stoop
I will do as I will,
either as act as act,
or dream for the sake of dreams,
and if they find me out
in rocket ships or jets
working to get away,

then let my left great-toe-
nail grow into the inside knob
of my right ankle-bone and let
my fingernails make eight new moons
temporarily in the cold salt marshes of my palms!
THIS IS THE WAY IT IS, and if
it is "a terrible disgrace"
it is as I must will,
because I am not them
though I am theirs to kill.

FRAGMENT ON THE
BRITISH MUSEUM

Confusedly, I used to think
of the wind as the item
connoting evanescence, and of stone
as the permanent thing, but
stone is blown full of holes
by the wind. The fighters' toes
in the Halicarnassus frieze
are corrupt with the athlete's foot
of many years of endurance,
or with some other wasting power.
Elgin! Where are the penises
and noses? A Captain Hammond
took two heads to Denmark;
other heads cut in half
show how the stone's brains
are full of incidents. Who cares
whether the faces are chopped off
or not? The fine grains of the stone
in the inside of their heads
are full of reasonable patterns.
The stone thought of the stone
figures is thus exposed:

that the marble is
processional like its friezes
of gods, people and beasts
and their grasses fed by water
down from the rock tables
in the mountains where
the marbles came from in
their process from the quarry
to the dust-motes in a sunbeam
entering a dead museum
and goes off someplace else
I can not know about while going.

ON BREEDING, FROM PLUTARCH

After the victory he loped
through town, still bloodily
unwounded, grinning like a dog
aroused, and with his sword
hanging down from his hand.
The Spartans yelled, "Go screw
What's-her-name just as you are,
crazy and stinking with war!
Her husband will be proud
or say he is, when she,
yielding, conceives a noble child."

POEM

Whatever was living is dead
and a lot of what was dead
has begun to move around,
so who knows what
the plan for a good state
is: they all go out
on the roads! Wherever
they came from is down,
wherever they're going
is not up yet, and everything
must make way, so,
now is the time to plan
for a new city of man.
The sky at the road's-end
where the road goes up
between one hill and ends,
is as blank as my mind,
but the cars fall off
into great plains beyond,
so who knows what
the plan for a good state
is: food, fuel, and rest
are the services, home
is in travel itself,
and burning signs at night
say DYNAFLO! to love,
so everything goes.

ON AN ACCIDENT:
ON A NEWSPAPER STORY

When a child turned in a false
alarm, a deaf man walked in front
of the fire engine. The attraction
between deafness and clangor is so
powerful, and some drivers are so
Christ-like—in saving the one
they damage many—that ten
people went to Coney Island Hospital
to lie as culls of the event among
the other victims of the Whip,
the Cyclone, and the Tunnel of Love.
Children can act largely, death
can be small, and art can go on
from the pains of its individuals.

851

A flying pigeon hit me on a fall day
because an old clothes buyer's junk cart
had surprised it in the gutter: license 851.
The summer slacks and skirts in the heap
looked not empty and not full of their legs,
and a baseball cap remained in head-shape.
Death is a complete collector of antiques
who finds, takes, and bales each individual
of every species all the time for sale to god,
and I, too, now have been brushed by wings.

FABRICATION OF ANCESTORS

For old Billy Dugan, shot in the ass in the Civil War,
my father said.

The old wound in my ass
has opened up again, but I
am past the prodigies
of youth's campaigns, and weep
where I used to laugh
in war's red humors, half
in love with silly-assed pains
and half not feeling them.
I have to sit up with
an indoor unsittable itch
before I go down late
and weeping to the storm-
cellar on a dirty night
and go to bed with the worms.
So pull the dirt up over me
and make a family joke
for Old Billy Blue Balls,
the oldest private in the world
with two ass-holes and no
place more to go to for a laugh
except the last one. Say:
The North won the Civil War
without much help from me
although I wear a proof
of the war's obscenity.

AUTUMN AT BAIAE: FOR CAVAFY

The women, clients, and slaves wept
and pretended the louder as he read
the temporal restitution of his thefts,
but the men stared: panic and avarice
exploded behind their eyes, shaded
from the candidate for certain lightning.
"Now, being condemned to a glory I
can neither avoid nor survive, I make
my will." Then, like a combat officer
committed for the last time to the point
of fire, M. C. Tacitus drove away
for his two hundred days as Emperor.

RIDING SONG FOR A SEMI-FEUDAL ARMY, FOR GLUBB PASHA, FOR TORTURED COLONELS

On a brilliant morning in May
we stole horses and set out
after the enemy (six kibbutzniks
gossiping about their tractors,
tractors and trivia), tired as usual
and dirty, but laughing and talking
of love. Then the poet of the left
flushed a quail, shot it through the eye,
jumped a rock-pile, caught it
as it fell, and gave it to the Colonel, saying:

"On a brilliant morning in May
we stole horses and set out
after the enemy (six kibbutzniks
debating the yokelization
of the intelligentsia). We were dirty and tired
as usual, but we laughed and talked
dirtily of love. Then I shot
a bird in the eye, caught it as it fell
so as to save the flesh intact
and gave it to the Colonel, saying:

'Who knows who will be alive
tomorrow? In the meantime I will give
the Colonel the bird to make him
able in strategy, careful in tactics, and
respectful of these lives of ours,
not that they matter: he
deserves a good last supper tonight.' "
The Colonel accepted the gift, laughing,
and turned to the war correspondent
riding beside him and said, "Now

you see why I like to sneak out
of the office and ride with these kids."
"I see," said the reporter. "It is vanity."
"The Colonel got the bird," said the poet.
"And we rode on after the enemy (six
kibbutzniks debating Martin Buber's so-called position),
fooling away our fear and dreaming
of peace and glory at the same time,
which is impossible, though death is not:
the Israelis are anti-romantic."

POEM

In the old days either the plaintiff or the defendant won or lost
justly or unjustly according to the mood of the court; the innocent
and the guilty were acquitted or condemned according to their luck
or pull with justice. Nowadays they are all condemned to death
by hard labor, together with the lawyers, juries, and arresting police.
Then the boards of review condemn the presiding judges too,
for having wasted time. In this way, all those who are in any way
connected with justice are impartially disconnected, and the clerk
closes the court house to join the last judgement. This is not to say
that there is no more justice: as an only natural human invention to
begin with, it has turned into the needs of the state, which needs labor
The whole apparatus can be forgotten in the absence of individuals
to whom to apply it, and the sensible man will have nothing to do
with anything outside his inner, passional life except his position.

ON LINES 69–70, BOOK IV,
OF VIRGIL'S *AENEID*

AENEAS: *Then I will found a temple of solid marble to*
Phoebus and Trivia.

You can read the pictures stamped
on the brass door: there
is Aeneas in chin and black boots
doing the Roman salute
as Dido tears at her hair.
The curly waves of the sea
perform close-order drill
while the purple corpse of Pan
disorders the public air
to show that Christ is here.
Long bugles of government
blow to their hearts' content
that honor is murderous.
I even saw Orpheus
sailing in Jason's fleet
and plucking a civic lyre
in praise of colonial fleece.
"That's enough," the priestess said.
"You came here in holy dread
and do not have the time
to laugh at the art any more.
I enlist whatever is mine,
so come in and fill out the forms."

ADMONITOR:
A PEARL FOR ARROGANCE

In winter a crow flew at my head
because her fledgling warmed
the brute nest of my fist. Ah,
the pearl clipped in her yellow beak
fell from her cry of "Ransom," and
I freed my bird for grace.

There in the pearl I prophesied
a ball to gaze in, with the stars
mirrored upon it as it held
the image of the crow at core.
Spread-eagled in the royal orb,
the black bird grew, one foot
holding lightning and the other,
worms: a herald arrogance.
I saw my fortune, iridescent
with deceit, my golden mask
the operative profile on a coin
haloed in motto: Order Reigns,
and backed by pestilent wings.

The window in this easter egg
exposed the blood's close tenement
where out-sized eyes, two bright
black pebbles in tarred grass,
were imminent with birth,
and hunger's instrument, the beak,
armored its hinterland of flesh
with bone. It will crack out
of art, the image at full term,
and cast about for meal.

How I hoped for a peaceable bird,
foolish as the gooney or dove!,
that would crack out of will
unhungry but immune to fists,
but I expect some arrogance
in flesh, be it of pigeons
or flightless birds, and do not know
a trustable source of order in
designs. I hear of Yeats' trick,
autocratic in the metal,
and of Picasso's normative dove,
gala with hopes, but what I eat
is this admonitory crow.

GENERAL PROTHALAMION
IN POPULOUS TIMES

Air is the first international
when soldiers smell the girls
and funerals in flowers in
contained wars in spring. They swear
allegiance to the air and are
remobilized for the campaigns
of love nightly, in sexual cells,
subverted by the nose to be
patriots of what is not
or partisans of a rose,
but go on drilling. So, fall out
on sick-call for a shot
against the air and go on
killing. A private Eden blooms
like a grenade inside their skulls,
corporal with apples, snakes, and Eves,
exploding outward toward the fall
from summer's marching innocence
to the last winter of general war.

THE CRIMES OF BERNARD

They were always arguing that we
were either the Devil's puppets or
God's marionettes, so when I said,
"What's the difference?, the latter
has us by the long hairs, the former
by the short, the best thing
about Commedia dell'Arte is
improvisation," they said, "There
are only two sides to a question: to
propose a third is treason if true.
Traitors we snatch bald, we
cut off their balls, we set them out
naked on the road to nowheres
as two-bit Abélards, two-bit whores,
and go on arguing as before."

ON VISITING CENTRAL PARK ZOO

The animals, hanging around in forms,
are each resigned to be what each one is,
imprisoned twice, in flesh first, then in irons.
The Bactrian camel is adjusted or is not
as, with his humps collapsed for lack of need
for water and with useless tufts of hair
like hummocks on the great plains of his flanks,
he stands around in shape and chews
a curd of solace, whether bitter, bland, or sweet,
who knows? Such is his formal pride,
his gargoyle's face remains a stone
assertion as he pisses in between his splayed,
seemingly rachitic legs and stays
that way, in place, for want of something else
to do, caught in his double prison all the time.
Whatever he is, he goes on being what he is,
although ridiculous in forced review,
perseverant in not doing what he need not do.

THE LIFE AND DEATH
OF THE CANTATA SYSTEM

When the Lord was a man of war and sailed out
through the sky at night with all the stars
of all the constellations as his riding lights,
those beneath his oceanic, personal ascendancy
ascended in fated systems. The massed shouts
of the chorus sailed a regular sea of violins
as Galleons of the Line!, with hulls of bassos,
decks of baritones and altos, ornate in poop
and prow in rigging up the masts of soloists
which bore aloft, in turn, soprano mainsails,
top-gallants of the children's chorus, and
pennants of castrati streaming on the heights!
The Great Armada sang "Invincible!" to the deep,
but when the time came for a change in craft
the Lord's storms wrecked the vessels of the Lord
and the voices poured out on the air still singing.
The Empirical English conquered in the shallows. He
withdrew his stars to favor those made by machines.

PLAGUE OF DEAD SHARKS

Who knows whether the sea heals or corrodes?
The wading, wintered pack-beasts of the feet
slough off, in spring, the dead rind of the shoes'
leather detention, the big toes' yellow horn
shines with a natural polish, and the whole
person seems to profit. The opposite appears
when dead sharks wash up along the beach
for no known reason. What is more built
for winning than the swept-back teeth,
water-finished fins, and pure bad eyes
these old, efficient forms of appetite
are dressed in? Yet it looks as if the sea
digested what it wished of them with viral ease
and threw up what was left to stink and dry.
If this shows how the sea approaches life
in its propensity to feed as animal entire,
then sharks are comforts, feet are terrified,
but they vacation in the mystery and why not?
Who knows whether the sea heals or corrodes?:
what the sun burns up of it, the moon puts back.

FROM HERACLITUS

Matter is palsy: the land heaving, water
breaking against it, the planet whirling
days in night. Even at the still point
of night I hear the jockeying for place
of each thing wrestling with itself
to be a wrestler. Is the stress that holds
them, whirling in themselves, an ache?
If so strained to shape and aching for release,
explode to peace! But I am here poised
within this eddy, sentenced to a shape,
and have to wrestle through a gust of violence
before I sleep; so may I make or augment
all these lights at night, so as to give out
all the temporary ornaments I can to peace.

ON FINDING THE
MEANING OF "RADIANCE"

The dreamed Grail found as if in dreams
was not as had been dreamed when found.
The blasted pot, so early in the earth
that it was nearly dirt in dirt, was fired
either in a kiln or a volcano: who can tell
a thumb or tool mark from an earthquake's
pressure in time, and what's the difference?
It is all part of the same process. In
the crater of the natural or potter's pot
there still is some of the first fluid.
It is, and why not say it, Perceval?,
piss-like, with a float of shit on top,
body and blood having changed in time
to what the beasts give back to the ground
with their personalities. Once drained,
the treasure is there in the lees, changed.
The gold filigree, once dreamed to be
a fine vein in the ore with the ore removed,
has run back into its rock, and the gems,
chipped facet by facet from their shells,
are back fast in their stones again, asleep;
but the gold lightning and jewels of fire
are freed in the finding of them, freed
by the nauseous draught: the fire balled
in the skull, the lightning veining the veins.
So I am freed to say, as a piece of dirt
to the body of earth: "Here is where love is,"
and, "This is the meaning of 'Radiance'."

A GIFT'S ACCOMPANIMENT

The central stone is small, small,
refractive, faceted, and red,
but small because of costs;
oh I can give no larger. Be
distracted from the jewel
which is so small by all
the craft of filigree around it:
it has been worked: it holds
a one night's curiosity
of intertwining stems and leaves,
radiant in ivy from the stone
which is so small. Look at
its corolla: the silvered multiple
details, man-houred craftily
around that stone, are by
love's labors a disguise
of poverty's small heart,
in hopes the saying is a lie
that says: "Small hearts evoke
small fates and no delights."
See how the spider-legged clasp
is soldered practically in back
so you (if you accept it though
the stone, expense, and heart
are small because of costs)
could wear it on the dress
you wear around the chest
you wear around your heart.
Please be the setting of
the setting of the setting of
this heart which is so small
though I can give no larger.

ARGUMENT TO LOVE AS A PERSON

The cut rhododendron branches
flowered in our sunless flat.
Don't complain to me, dear,
that I waste your life in poverty:
you and the cuttings prove: Those
that have it in them to be beautiful
flower wherever they are!, although
they are, like everything else, ephemeral.
Freedom is as mortal as tyranny.

IN THE FOREST

it was warm and cold,
cold from the damps because
it all took place in trees.
When it rained it rained
and when the rain stopped
the trees rained in the wind
and when the trees stopped
it rained. So it went.

Once it was huddling, once
it was sitting apart, once
it was bleeding in time.
We ate and we drank
and we slept and we
did something else
we should not talk about.
Was it love? It was all
supposed to be love.

My it was dark
at night. Whoever it was
who planned that place
forgot the lighting
although some claim to see.

A SAWYER'S RAGE AGAINST
TREES NOBLE AS HORSES

1.

Inwardly centered like a child
sucking soda through a straw,
they have their noses in the dirt,
greedily absent, blinded, while
their green behinds in the wind
wave back and forth. Oh I can
hit them and they won't hit back.
Oh let them all come down, slowly at the first inclination from
the vertical, then faster, then
crashing in passion! There is
a hallelujah from the dust and birds,
and insects are set free of hell
in devilish shapes to shrivel in
the solid glare of the day, fools
to the contrary, who maintain
that Christ is down from the heights
by this, to the mother earth again.

2.

It is even, the way the trees,
in coming up from the ground,
from nothing, from a nut,
take liberties in spreading out
like animals, like us. But, brutes
of a chosen ground, they stand
around in suction, dark, grouped
like witnesses afraid to act
beside the accidents of roads
and more afraid to cross except
packed in a squirrel's cheek,
in nuts, or in a fairy's flight
of seed. Their undersides are dark
in contrast to the strong, blond,
human inner arm; even the ground
beneath them is a hairy damp,
dirty as groins. Oh we will cut
them down to boards, pulp, dust
and size: fury the ax, fury the saw
will cure their spreading stands;
courage will make the world plain.

WHAT THE HELL, RAGE,
GIVE IN TO NATURAL GRACES

She walks. This never has
been done before. She shows
how it is done: her forearms
raised, waving her hands
on the natural rachets of her wrists,
she takes steps! She balances
on black spike heels so sharp
that they would pierce your heart
if she could walk on you,
and smiles to show it off:
this is a giddy new art
she owns squealing because
she steps on certain things—
spittle and cigarette butts
littered from some past—
and comes back from the store
with the first ice-cream cone
in the whole world to date,
her walking being as light
as my irony is heavy.
She blinks rapidly when
she tells me all this because
wild insects of perception get
into her eyes and bite them.
Thinking of history, oh I
must speak of What's-her-name,
sweet sixteen and never been

and never will be, just is;
but speak of love and she's
a sweet one to the senses,
palpably adequate, e-
motionally to be husbanded
because the world is weird
because it's here while she
is. Yesterday would surprise
her if she heard of it,
as will tomorrow when she does,
or else not. As of now,
things are for the first
and last time timeless like
the Classic Comic strips
and known to her agreeably
except for stepped-on things
littered from some past,
so what the hell, rage,
give in to native graces:
her brains are in her tits!,
as she knows bouncingly,
and there for all to love,
since the world fights its war
in her womb and so far wins.

ON TREES

SECULAR METAMORPHOSIS OF
JOYCE KILMER'S "TREES"

Don't talk to me about trees having branches and roots:
they are all root, except for the trunk, and the high root,
waving its colors in the air, is no less snarled in its food
than is the low root snarled in its specialty: nourishment
in dirt. What with the reciprocal fair trade of the trunk
holding the two roots together and apart in equipoise,
the whole tree stands in solid connection to its whole self
except for the expendable beauty of its seasonal ends,
and is so snarled at either end in its contrary goods
that it studs the dirt to the air with its living wood.
This anagogic significance grows with its growth for years,
twigging in all directions as an evidence of entirety,
although it waves back and forth in the wind and is a host
to fungi, insects, men, birds, and the law of entropy.

POEM

What was once an island with birds,
palms, snakes, and goats in flowers
is now a sand-bar bearing sea-clams.
A storm at sea washed over it and it
drowned. There is no food but what
the surf throws up to it and no sweet
water but what the sky throws down.
You are cast away one storm too late
to know the previous ecology,
so may you leave it soon, or fertilize
the sand-bar for another kind of life:
you can do nothing except your part
unless you want a short survival badly.
So what if you act like a storm against
sweet water, other castaways, and clams?
They will give out!, as you will, soon:
no more interrelational elegance
will burgeon on this desert in the sea,
and no prayers make it bear analogies.

MONOLOGUE OF A
COMMERCIAL FISHERMAN

"If you work a body of water and a body of woman
you can take fish out of one and children out of the other
for the two kinds of survival. The fishing is good,
both kinds are adequate in pleasures and yield,
but the hard work and the miseries are killing;
it is a good life if life is good. If not, not.
You are out in the world and in in the world,
having it both ways: it is sportive and prevenient living
combined, although you have to think about the weathers
and the hard work and the miseries are what I said.
It runs on like water, quickly, under the boat,
then slowly like the sand dunes under the house.
You survive by yourself by the one fish for a while
and then by the other afterward when you run out.
You run out a hooky life baited with good times,
and whether the catch is caught or not is a question
for those who go fishing for men or among them for things."

VARIATION ON A
THEME BY STEVENS

In fall and whiskey weather when
the eye clears with the air and blood
comes up to surface one last time
before the winter and its sleeps,
the weeds go down to straws,
the north wind strips most birds
out of the atmosphere and they
go southward with the sunlight,
the retired people, and rich airs.
All appetites revive and love
is possible again in clarity
without the sweats of heat: it makes
warmth. The wall-eyed arctic birds
arrive to summer in the fall,
warmed by these chills; geese
practice their noisy "V"s,
half a horizon wide, and white owls
hide from their crows in the pines.
Therefore it is not tragic to stay
and not tragic or comic to go,
but it is absolutely typical to say
goodbye while saying hello.

FROM ROME. FOR MORE PUBLIC FOUNTAINS IN NEW YORK CITY

Oh effervescent palisades of ferns in drippage,
the air sounds green by civic watered bronze
fountains in New York City. Hierarchs of spray
go up and down in office: they scour the noons
when hot air stinks to itself from Jersey's smoke
and the city makes itself a desert of cement.
Moses! Command the sun to august temperance!
When water rises freely over force and poises,
cleaning itself in the dirty air, it falls back
on the dolphins, Poseidon, and moss-headed nymphs,
clean with the dirt of air left cleansed by its
clear falling, and runs down cooly with the heat
to its commune, pooling. What public utility!
The city that has working fountains, that lights
them up at night electrically, that does not say
to thirsters at its fountains: DO NOT DRINK!—
that city is well ordered in its waters and drains
and dresses its corruption up in rainbows, false
to the eye but how expressive of a cool truth being.
The unitary water separates, novel on its heights,
and falls back to its unity, discoursing. So let
New York City fountains be the archives of ascent
that teach the low high styles in the open air
and frondage of event! Then all our subway selves
could learn to fall with grace, after sparkling,
and the city's life acknowledge the water of life.

ACCOMMODATION TO DETROIT

"When good people die they become worms in Detroit," they say.
"When bad people die they go to Hamtramck just as they are."
It is all right to mock it, but some are exalted: they
have escaped to the cities from the bad-lands to the south
and see them as their Edens found, with Eves and the fruits
and shelter under iron trees. They have had a hard life
as draught animals, and are here to try out human life,
temptations first. They are walled away from their wilderness
by absence in stone and iron, the way Hamtramck is walled
by Detroit, city in city, cement in cement, and seed in shell.
Greater Detroit is what has grown around the ones who have
Hamtramck or nothing as a preview of a concrete flower to come.

TO PARIS: FEAR OF THE
HEIGHTS REACHED

Oh I came up from anywhere
from underground, brushing the dirt
from my hair and knees, and climbed
the long stalk of the road until
it flowered in confusing petals. I
thought I was lost in its light
shadows, in confusion of ways
and absence of felt pattern. I hoped
to find a way back out again
but was so lost I found
the heart, place, square, monoliths and fountains
bleeding with honey out of which the city grew,
bowing away in plan, petal on petal,
as a chrysanthemum of sunlight.
Oh I felt out its day's commitment
to the sun, and how it shone itself
throughout one night. There was
the sky above it, high although
the flower of the city was up high.
Oh I stayed out the cycle of its day,
drunk on its juices, sneezing its dust,
and shaken by the order and complexity.
I was convinced that it was beautiful
but left it: it was not for me,
so I came off it and am back
down where I came from on the ground.

STABILITY BEFORE DEPARTURE

I have begun my freedom and it hurts.
Time opens out, so I can see its end
as the black rock of Mecca up ahead.
I have cut loose from my bases of support
and my beasts and burdens are ready, but
I pace back and forth across my right
of way, shouting, "Take off! Move out
in force!", but nothing moves. I wait
for a following storm to blast me out of here
because to go there freely is suicide!
Let the wind bear my responsibility.

WINTER: FOR AN
UNTENABLE SITUATION

Outside it is cold. Inside,
although the fire has gone out
and all the furniture is burnt,
it is much warmer. Oh let
the white refrigerator car
of day go by in glacial thunder:
when it gets dark, and when
the branches of the tree outside
look wet because it is so dark,
oh we will burn the house itself
for warmth, the wet tree too,
you will burn me, I will burn you,
and when the last brick of the fireplace
has been cracked for its nut of warmth
and the last bone cracked for its coal
and the andirons themselves sucked cold,
we will move on!, remembering
the burning house, the burning tree,
the burning you, the burning me,
the ashes, the brick-dust, the bitter iron,
and the time when we were warm,
and say, "Those were the good old days."